She's My Best Friend

She's My Best Friend

poems by Jim Behrle

2006 : Pressed Wafer : Boston

for Gerrit Lansing

"Breakwater" originally appeared in *Surgery of Modern Warfare*, thanks to Amy Fusselman. "Good Night, All You Ships At Sea, You" originally appeared in the SPD catalog (thanks to Elizabeth Treadwell Jackson) and then later in the Subpress anthology *Free Radicals* edited by Jordan Davis and Sarah Manguso. Thanks to them.

"Sense of Milieu" uses one line from every poet in *The New American Poetry* (edited by Donald Allen), "Psalm" uses one line alphabetically from Stuart Z. Perkoff's *Voices of the Lady: Collected Poems*, and "How Am I to Convince You?" borrows one line from some of the poets in *Legitimate Dangers* edited by Cate Marvin and Michael Dumanis.

ISBN: 0-9785156-0-9
ISBN 13: 978-0-9785156-0-7

typeslowly designed

Cover photograph by Ben E. Watkins

Printed in Michigan by Cushing-Malloy, Inc.

Pressed Wafer / 9 Columbus Square / Boston, MA 02116

Contents

Beacon Arms

from this moment on, what is
    To be Left Behind?
          bread crumbs, post-its

Should I get married and be Good or puke?

       Trample and buzz forward Solo.

Upon reading this Maybe you'll feel less chased
       I gotta go. *You* gotta go?
       We better go.

Very brass, the stonework of the Morning After,

Is it wrong to blow the Students and Tourists?
       And who's asking the
       tough questions These days

Most don't remember birthdays. From now on
       we'll keep the gears
       clean.

There's a call on 1 or 2.

It's a future you, fucking with you now.

Going to the chapel, hunting cheap wine and eucharist

Becuz No One's looking and you can:
    induct magic into the Hall

Breakwater

a sparrow cannot be opened
or punched. exodus teaches us.
if I reached into you I would
get a no or a yes. what is
holding us up? love is not
a bargain. if you lived here
you'd be dead by now. so
would I. she used to work in a diner
beneath the hot lights and refill
drinks. why can't you be more
like her? without your bones
and muscles you're nothing:
a mixed drink. she is alive
in motion, wearing your silk shirt.
animals can't be punished or taken apart.
it's a fact: we rely on pullies,
we're forced to beget. let it
be me who chokes you like
you like it, with the alphabet.
unclean: go team.

Now Your Panties Fit Me

everybody stop and procreate!

no money kept on premesis

I hear the bells! I see Catherine's face!

must cultivate more fake online connections

read FASCICLE to me, I'm dreary!

we follow the moustache over the cliff

better get my assless chaps drycleaned

I shimmer in the universe I use shimmering ellipsis

we're poets of the middle we're *nervous*

I miss your body and want your new chapbook

it's an incredible morning here but obviously not in warzones

hey somehow always behaving well is *most* important

I am the hammer that melts the shimmering ice

"I'll be bored while you're gored / to death"

I was born with italics in my shimmering fist

I want somebody *RICH*/ with room to grow

not uncomfortable, with a little bow

Fresh Kills

Submerge and surrender to the Dopey
                        bliss

At least pedophiles have a Hobby

I'm hoping the horrible Bastards
                    will Speak my

Language or else come and Chew
It up

You are scamming on All the available
            Chicks with furious

hopes of Making progress, I
                falter at the goal line

hoping for divine Abdication

wear your purple Robes for subway
encounters

I'll wear pajamas or a
                Parachute for

Ferry rides on Garbage sloops

No difference has ever been Made
and No quarter granted

Count the steps it takes to
block Bills from

becoming laws, to Stop a
                desperate 2 point
                Conversion

We argue for the Status quo
                while we Wrestle

with Thoughtless change, drop

your pants to find a chrysalis

Haiku

Demanding that all the neon in town become black neon.
That this would need to happen overnight. Spirits laugh at
us for being alive. They have the best parking lots, built in
the air over rivers. The Nile for example. You couldn't stop
calling me, you became a telephone operator. They gather
in church halls to swear off the present. It's an everyday
struggle.

Daddy!

What the snakes possessed was
Astounding. They had gathered
Up all of our legs when we
Weren't paying attention. This
Made them dangerous, the snakes.
We were powerless to stop them
And we ourselves became snakes.
They had the advantage of
Having been snakes for much
Longer, and for having sewn
Our legs onto their bodies.
We were snakes with arms.
Have I mentioned their
Fangs? This was not a
Pleasant time if you weren't
Born a snake. Later we
Regretted writing poems about
It. Anthologies were burned
And replaced by haystacks,
Which also burned. Everything
Was fanged and very dangerous
As was previously mentioned.
Words were repeated and faded
Away, thanks to our dangerous foes

La Fille De La Mort

Undulate across my parse Spectrum for starters

Fingers are to be fought Off, plus

Some lady's gonna Choose you, but not yet
tho
Your kimino is *Ready* to be stained and torn

Cross sweepstakes with a Harbinger
to attest to the badness of Wealthy nations

Ice can be used as a Terrific metaphor
             while waiting to Be harshly
                  begrudged

Say: I never met a finer gentleman

  or

  I've been pimping All my life

They cuddle in the Valley of same difference

And will swallow the particles of hot Fog
             that will blow in soon

Tell them: No one seemed to want my Loving

or Heat then
        Reach for the shallow profanities

that express that Comfortable notion: you
                        and
                        Me
        anytime,   your place
mine
    everything must Go

.

Too Bruce Andrews / Too Victoria Secret

the happy childhood is *in effect*
I find your indifference incredibly erotic
the way you get to make a lover feel
between choking and
so it's my fault no one reads your blog
& who told you you get to feel so bullied
we ask God what the fuck
up come the fireflies to be snuffed
tell me you're packing heat
where did you get that sweet pitchfork
was perhaps mauled by a lion
the ones with husbands are all over me
I thought they were stars they are x's
so yellow close up

Taken as an Ominous Sign

coming up next on Cinemax
sweating at the tips
with a lap full of Ophelia
after some Olson twins Aqua Fresh
a beautiful dead owl on the traintracks
I think I lost an earring inside you
in this fantasy an ostrich
and Jackie's still my favorite poet
set free thru the text
demanding the universe *astonish* me
minus the scare quotes
while breaking in a rookie partner

Sestina *for Anonymous*

pentagons only keep sponsors alive
burn victims in fishbowls of milk

the poisonous point at horizons
stuffed like bras, shockingly red

culture has shorted the register
for the last time *ever* tonite,

a curb calls the woebegotten into
actions that'll please weak opposition

interiors cry out to be made
garish, to glint impoverished void

get the vig, let's pow-wow
near the couch, velvets face

bricks, those future haystacks

Maggie Gyllenhaal's Knees

she's a delight at all times

having photoshopped the orgasm

Korean graffitti cat tell me your secrets

if the revolution isn't on Fox News

so why are my hands shaking

& you realized you were in love with Jackie

diet Dr. Pepper in Spiderman's eye

we met at a jaws of life party

if you see something unusual or suspicious

some characters may be lost

do you want to be in the pome?

yeah but neurotic in a hot way

the kind of girl you can meet in a bar

Carry your grief alone
Cedar and jagged fir
Down on the flat of the lake
Each pale Christ stirring underground
Easily to the old
Encompassed by a thousand nameless fears
Far voices
Fine gold is here; yea, heavy yellow gold
Fly away, away, swallow

For eyes he waved greentipped
For hours the princess would not play or sleep

From plains that reel to the southward, dim
From stone to bronze, from bronze to steel

From where I sit, I see the stars

Hearing the strange night-piercing sound
Here by the gray north sea
In the narrow room there is no light

Southpaw

for John Mulrooney

deathwish never looked so Hot,
          a favorite number of ours

During intercourse it's funny to hum
          "Helter Skelter" or to ask
          for more meatloaf

It's no longer enough to cry Uncle, or to be
whisked away to a quiet place to be
          Beaten

Father used my belt to tie my hands
     in the closet, I now
          leave it to Gravity

          to select my Toppings

You are made of fiery tattoos and have Been fire
          twice, I lick

the sink and tub for final mescaline Specks.

Pay-per-view home invasions and
     crude interludes in cars
        will be Next

Followed by Dumpster Divers already
in Progress
I wish I could say "Second Avenue" or
"Houston St."

Instead we fall into Suburban traps that
will toughen skins

A shame you have become Microscopic
to have thrown in your tiny towel

Shrinking and too tired to Matter

Love comes to the serial killers, their
relentless murderous mistakes

Why I Am Not "Post-Avant"

the cliff notes said so

for I do not come after you

I just came and now must wait a while

thus Paris Hilton gets to be in the poem

& livejournal teaches us about the kitty

a vague memory of getting wet

history books ain't written by the conquered
& you only get to name your kids or pets
objects succumb, at peace with being pushed out
so when the poet said pubic hair

I imagined her pubic hair

which only her husband gets to see

a list of things to say to the steady cam

the uneven distribution of particles

upon your face / some damage

falling in sunbeam at departure
because they used every beautiful thing up

the Jem'Hadar surrender also the dirty ocean birds

despite our manifestos teach us to humor
the elders we must bear

black flag, please twist above the *Targét*

Pixie Says

let us undermine the bourgeoisie

sounds like we've been eating poison berries

the wheel of love comes to rest in the field of love

on nights such as this

callback numbers violate our blood oaths

thrilled you say? yes *thrilled*

Jacqueline, we're still recovering from

a visit by the ugliest bird in the world

anyone can leave comments to this entry

so no France no funny

oh half-naked green witch of the sea

you are delicious and I love you

expand all

when you're nice it gives me a stiffy

Point Guard of the Future

You are talented at boring. / Freeze and be implicated / For
many felonies. It's a / Fun new dance: the Sleepwalk. / Put
your hands on your / Hips. Those aren't your hips. / Wander
through watercolors, in / search of an original timepiece. /
Why you so blue? It's the / Fresh new craze. It's written / On
your eyes, you want me. / C'mon, feel the pumping organs /
And feel the stomach. That's / Your baby brother, a / Highly
regarded cheeseburger. / I will translate us from / Poor to
Wealthy. Seconds / Come off back off the / Clock. I'm trying
to remember / Anything you ever did. / Liars built the pyramids,
Stone / By stone. I am ready to be popular / Prepared to be
rewarded. / Watch out university, here's / Johnny needing love.

Ortiz Has a Posse

who so loved the world

but never spoke to us again

build a cage of cocks

baby I want you to fill the sky

but not in a fat way

still working out that cock image

kid reading CATCHER IN THE RYE
probably wants to kill the President

just trying to imagine everyone's sex face

all the time or gets to lament

I just want you around when I orgasm

rubber bullets get in your eyes

be well in the land of the crab

Haiku

I saw your feet on the stairs and then instantly liked you,
stranger. Your blouse was orange, I think. Call me at work,
617 354 5201. Memos went to the movies, hands sweaty. I'm
not a feet guy, I don't want you to think that. In warehouses
pens exploded. We invented food. Elaborate excuses were
made and accepted skeptically. There never were any stairs.
Someone's opening the door and talking.

Good Night, All You Ships at Sea, You

for Geneva Chao

We're on Sorrow Watch engulfed by Scorpion Bowls

haunted repeatedly in Dreams by Dave Letterman

when it's my funeral I'll want La Cucachá
                   and F-16 flyovers

First choose your weight in water: essence
                     of mango or Youth

No one dies with you, regardless of riches
                   or recent poll numbers

Ex-girlfriends gather to march huffily Toward shore

Adapting to the new Ban on hullabaloo

At the first signs   Yet agape, Shudder to think of

Inflamed tonsils, they Strike
              You down walking your Delightful coast

Dateline Egypt: Could have had more Pyramids
if only we'd Worked together

Pass a bottle of Nile, while watching soldiers fortify
every Ferris Wheel or Tilt-a-Whirl

O to be the one To chase off the Frankensteins
              we built

Hooray for our impossible Demands,
shrugged off   Undershirt   and clean Sheets misplaced

Starts with a Line from Jeni Olin

"by beautiful I mean communicating disease"

hoped they might be hissing like snakes

it's in my panties / the secrets like

the prophecies are all coming true like

that erotic one

the tip of my dick made a fetus briefly

free memory upgrade / a loop of just Paris Hilton

mark of the beast carry the one

our nerf sex dungeon / avengers in the house

I could be the perfect girl but not for you

I thought it was love it was a gas leak

winning them over is only worth 50 points

we had to leave the country in a hurry

your back against a mens room stall c'mon

Psalm

A man who worships flesh
Behind my transparent wall
Can't see it.
Difficult to be human.
Everything comes eventually
Face to face. Is the gun.
Go to the huge prison.
His destiny the inevitable rot.
I am thinking about Kenneth Patchen,
Junk nursery rhymes
Kites & airplanes & birds
Lined up against the wall in twos.
Making a poem out of bodies.
Nothing of me needs poems small
Over my prayer shattered head.
Poets of the world be careful.
See my dead eye.
The killers swarm the city.
Undetected I am.
We have here clumsy hands.
You say we are together in this house.
Thunder of fucking and horns.

Poem from Deep in the Womb

don't everyone answer at once

who ignited the desire machines?

cycle of violence plays out over the

semi-conscious body of Katie Holmes

graffiti says TRY NOT TO DIE AGAIN

to fill you up with these songs

flip the switch bitch

spoken in fuckwhispers it's

daybreak over Jehovahtown

is captured by a renegade telepath.

good morning security cameras

I'm from New York now sit on my face

to live in Astor Place inside

a new scary mirror

must smell like crotch all the time

the bell of my throat bongs Jacqueline, Jacqueline

read me the *Iliad* / do *all* the voices

Direwood

Suddenly they've slipped our flank: red foxes.
Stumbling, hungover, wobbly as fresh foals.

Whiskey-breathed, delirious creatures, hot
Eyes and ears, circling to sniff fingers in shake.

Out their jackknives will streak, our cold leather
Will be theirs tonight. Half moon for a jester.

Owls whoop, having assembled, puffing at wet
Camels, ready to catch our late show's curtains.

Leaves report our sweating as metronome-steady
Crunch, calm as harvest's gust. Does whistle

From slick embraces, rattling at antler in a fever.
Glass snap, clearly hoof to vial. So quivers blood

In each direction, mostly rising. Beneath the pines
Saliva rises like rough laughter, from the spinning gut.

You Are a Part of the Thing I Want

give my regards to Gitmo

dog which is also a bird

the o on your eyeballs

stands for override

a kiss that turns to a cobra

in the mouth of an android

we survived the great fire of Cairo

having lost only 100 hit points

getting ever wistful for anthrax

better call to cancel the stripper cake

G. Apollinaire is alive in the

mischievous faces of Bruno and Bobo

maybe needing caterpillar for the upper lip

I endure as a poet to sleep with poets

if only I'd been a complete douchebag

we'd be on the Upper Peninsula by now

with a daughter named Sluggo

everything gets clearer after a blow to the groin

Stopping By Woods on a Snowy Evening

I like getting fucked

as a way of encouraging dialogue

during the dream of Thaya

don't ask for my password for 2 weeks

it will happen if you say yes

war criminals in the house say hell yeah

Europe loves our dowdy spinsters

bye bye bong / "I don't need to satisfy tonight"

ready for the spectacular car chase

hussy of the lowlands peeled off the label

turned vixen and prancer to glue

just me and my microphone

sometimes people recognize themselves in my poems

covered in redi-whip

suffering beneath a Western sky

Self-Convex Oath on a Tennis Court

vote for a black pope

can almost smell the masking agents

you have been banned from this forum

guess who needs medicine

I'd love to throw up in your hair

car chase of the improved *Lolita*

because we love freedom *so fucking much*

kiss the barcode free Judas Iscariot

by Grand Central Station I shot a hooker

beat the sonogram endangered species takeout

I saw the greatest minds of my generation sell out

memoirs for moms on mescaline

I can keep it brotherly

she brought my underwear to the bookstore in a Duane
Reade bag

alchemy alchemy alchemy teeth

5th Avenue is all rosaries & crucifixes

the images keep coming

chemicals inside an oriole

after being such a happy baby

Sense of Milieu

I mark him zero & mine
& love is an evil word.
I threw 6 bucks away
In the dawn that is nowhere.
Tonight and forever I shall be yours
Continually re-learning the same words.
Light bounces off mossy rocks down to me.
It's the shape of a tulip.
The language itself has wings.
We sweat past each other
She in whose lipservice
That the impossible distance
Swaggering and dying is
More beautiful than the world. He is
Enough to poison the heart,
And he rattled teeth in my pelvis.
They gesticulate nervously and it's London,
God feeds on god
I go separately.
I hide and wait like a naked child
Belly gold so bright you'd swear he had
Warm bloodgiving flesh.
Even here the young loves
Leave the world alone, it is dangerous.
Or how she looks and says yea
Against the coming of guests.

I saw an animal in the park.
That I hold converse with your fantasy.
To the poet who works up everything
Imprint of flexible mouth sounds
So much more than mere mankind.
Those left will be gods and seraphim.
At her sides there are long wings, folded.
I try to warn them that it's really me.
I have watched them, at night, dark and sad
And he is the flippy flesh made word.
Now the eyes look up.
Once this happened
You would understand
All things contain the seeds.
I swear the room is warm.
Oh to be seventeen years old
Maybe buy a piano or make fudge.
In the reality of anything.

This Is Also Your Return Envelope

language isn't poetry

yet / must be the same dress size

audience is the new orgasm

I behave abominably during the trailer

and everyone ends up in cobra position

do you want a bag with your dingoes?

pens down / pharmacies deliver us

the cute girl from the McGriddles commercial googled me

fragrance of a hyphen / ain't havin' it

"is the pathway to many abilities some consider to be unnatural"

my collected hoaxes rock your box

thoughts of Gerrit foreshadow the Stephen Jonas reference

ladies of Schermerhorn released into glamor

"you were the chosen one!"

when mind games that got delicious

became a prosody all Sith & Netflix

go on, waive your right to counsel

I've come to chew on *you*

Low Among the Cunt Flowers

tonight on the island of the easily-amused

hey kids, cue: fantasy

if I can't have Carol Mirakove I don't want nobody, baby

so who says Western Civilization is worth saving
or the earth

dangle your feet above the epicenter

and in this juxtaposition: Keanu

first thing this morning the drowned rat of the toilet

I got two oranges in my pocket, unmolested

Jacqueline's name has passed through me like a feast

now is the time to save over $500

thank God my computer is powered by semen

speak to the Bowery with your tinkle

I will arise and go to my father

but first I'm expecting a fax

leave a Stephanie for me, hunh?

blossoms devestate but there's

always a more beautiful woman elsewhere

one orange left, must be a trap

I Cried All the Way to the Altar

long into the night, too,
beneath your chin. your

stare makes me remember
the Alamo, and salute.

give me a million days
alone, give me cool water

or rum. lock me in a
terrible basement. don't

call me up for supper,
don't set a place. honey,
scratch my tired face.

B. Y. O. Beotch

the girl I was supposed to love

died on 9/11 or in Iraq probably

now a long velcro rip

ha and am quite a good spankee

so you've given up on Jackie

because maybe God's retarded

we spoon the ocean until bereft or midnite

whichever comes first

go commando onward

I am waving a moon-shaped flag

which is a terrible thing to do

Fear of Poetry

no american casualties to report yet

for the next wedding present

a candy made from cat piss

hey Soccer Mom buy *this*

canoe built out of John Godfrey poems

all of a sudden angels with chainsaws

the goose that glows glows for Bernadette

to the delight of the firefly demographic

here's a cool superhero nickname: Adulteress

although there's no need to go cannibal

we hanker for hippychick quesadilla

the poem walked into a bar

it didn't wanna die a virgin

as of today I'm 4th in All-Star balloting

the sky's the bedsheet no one wants to shrug off

washing up after a dream of Justice Scalia

sugarfree beneath default security

& for some reason I still want you to tear me apart

Her Name Is Apparently "Catastrophe"

Viva the wafer!

into the Year of the Unicorn I think

having thoroughly confounded Metropolix

which lives on the other side of the firewall

haven't you heard I'm your secret santa

those eyes not nearly bamboo enough

more alive than f-9 fixtures

every field of vision deserves stars

c'mon! more of a process blue

I thought I was freaking you out

some days even the cartoons seem *nervous*

so you'd like to become a first reader

commanding dark enough magick to hold snowballs together

thankfully my mutant power

no I meant that like my bald shiny head

bathes in the halo of you and your poems' goodness

nothing but sugar-rush a loop like the afterlife

fyi if the messengers ever show up

across the board cuts in the dream budget

for Monday forgive television and music

system preferences set on cobalt

especially during such dark times

on Avenue Cathedral they'll sell the sex tape

Sprinklers Throughout the Building

Sawako you were in my dream

And I am almost born

My mouth's such a sweet place

But I keep making mistakes

Lone blackbird the sky's underwear

Since I feel like bretraying you

Don't sleep with Lewis Warsh

Shaka, when the walls fell

Cuz you shine on me whereever you are

Poets trust angels too much

He's a quitter and I think that's sexy

Touch flowers at your own risk

New Outgoing Message

unless you'd rather hear about my grandmother

thank Christ you see thru my swagger

neighborhood kids boosted my halo & wings

haiku / hipbone / another hippocratic oath

why you being like this

I'll read Jennifer Moxley to you

O *Magnolia* Soundtrack

beneath the suds of dawn

kathunk goes the compliment

malfunctions inside anti-gravity

yeah like *you* could do better

things will be fine when there's less Americans

if you leave it blank it will be auto-generated

we douche & ditch

and the people shout *jed ne pivo*!

I put a needle on the record

we know where you're from

I just shot John Lennon

and the flesh cries Olivia!

that's not the fucking sun

guess tonite you left the club because

everything you want is wrong

that's the fist you're feeling

now that I'm famous

To My Valentine

For SM

I want what everyone wants.
The prongs of the vise,
a climbing italics of ardor.
Newsprint black beneath the eyes.
Sure, two shadows against the CVS.
Vanilla moves in love's lack-light,
Why not? Above all idle engines.
To hover at risk.
Pleasing you with only the black keys,
I am like someone in love.
Within I am more blue than red.
Songbirds at prayer, remember me.
I love the way dreamers love:
by accident, beneath haze.
Yes, tell them this is your song.
Written by the purple bird
who pecks upon your chest
with imaginary grace.
It is the prayer of that dark bird.
The air will lift and release.
I want to know what the dream knows:
what I love and why.
How copper suffers into green.
Air also forgives all sounds that ask.
The air decides what music is,

the air is the end of dreaming.
Valentine, let it choose what will shine
or fade.
Let it silence or swell.
Let it risk with light.

I Know Bush Sucks Quit Spamming Me

file under: they're gonna steal this election too
during this garnishment *damn* fool
I thought the ad said succubus
date your own fresh döppleganger
be the holy crap skeeball prize
responsible for countless erections
but if you cut the black wire I won't need anymore
whatever minutes
from your roof I see the stars are puppets
let's reference the X-Files
while stingers meet the altruistic maw
don't thank me from the podium
but how to shake the goo from my hand
and maintain my super-cool exterior

Haiku [for Jane Dark]

what ought to have been a lovely union of souls instead
became a food fight. Volkswagens drove over fences.
Impossible to find a coat at the bottom of the pile,
unrecognizable. I wanted to build a tractor. I wanted
us to build a tractor together. Diseases are built out of
a combination of factors we would not otherwise fear.
Suppressing the love we felt was the smartest thing. Have
some pie.

Tonight, with Two Stolen Lines from Franz Wright

"Through the beautiful quiet of tree sounds"

you are not prepared for the dream of Olena Kalytiak Davis

OK your cock grows swollen again

the tiresome things I have to do to my body to feel temporarily
aroused

"And contributing one's atoms to the green universe"

a green smoke rises from my feet

part of the post-Crush List/post-O-Jackie-love-me-back murk

from above a refreshing drop of air-conditioner schmoo

rest comes above the quim done wrong

anything would do / except what you *just* did

no not another "New Anything" for fucksakes

zygotes may yet learn to stomp my spleen

wither beneath their magnum cherry-flavored hogs

rough boys of the blog world simper

inside all the crazy boxes / instead it's cheese.com

great is the mercy of the lord no one

here seems to believe in / great are his deeds

touch me anywhere to release the rising goo

And how am I to convince you if you aren't here to
Convince?

Look you've won a Ghost Town

Which left some hours ago

Yes my captain, I

Was there

But what's the use of being pretty If I won't get better?

I want to be younger than I am
I am about to recite a psalm I know
And you will know what I told you is true
When another subway came I crawled on
I am going to fail light and stars and tears

For Catherine Meng, with Longing, & Three Stolen Lines from Jorie

"(what will you do next?)(—feel it beginning?)"

when they recover the black boxes they'll hear us say this

shrieking or whatever

in the life of this Bond villain

that thing you did to me at the opera / do *that* again

"(somewhere the castle above the river)"

don't discourage my nuclear ambitions

We're Free Radicals Forever!

we keyed your veritas / O Meg and Jack

I only gave you two stars

ruckus served all day

I read in a magazine that women only have

400 orgasms in their bodies to use over the course

of their lives / that can't be true

clap your hands / PEEP

we've never been this happy! is that healthy?

what to do with all these Perrier bottles?

"(somewhere you holding this piece of paper)"

from the people that brought you John Ashbunny

we're rocking the new planet they found

the Official Verse Culture can't keep me down

I'm anti-war

and Can You Handle the New Sincerity?

I can't handle the applause after poetry readings

I don't want it anymore

JIM BEHRLE's poems have appeared most recently in *Cannibal* and *The Tiny*. *(Purple) Notebook of the Lake* was released by Braincase Press in 2004 and he was featured in the anthology *Free Radicals: American Poets Before Their First Books.* Google him to discover his various web shenanigans.